ERECTRIC SCHLOCK

Lê

© Aimée Lê, 2022. All rights reserved; no part of this book may be reproduced by any means without the publisher's permission.

ISBN: 978-1-915079-15-2

The author has asserted their right to be identified as the author of this Work in accordance with the Copyright, Designs and Patents Act 1988

Cover design by Aaron Kent

Edited & Typeset by Aaron Kent

Broken Sleep Books (2022)

Broken Sleep Books Ltd
Rhydwen,
Talgarreg,
SA44 4HB
Wales

Contents

REJECTED BY SUBWAY FRANCHISE EMPLOYEES [...]	9
I HAVE THE SWAGGER OF A 17-YEAR-OLD	11
HOW IT GOING	12
WHY AM I ALWAYS FALLING OFF A CLIFF?	14
THE NATIONAL QUESTION IN 3 PARTS	16
MY INTERNATIONALE	18
PECHA KUCHA FOR THE PEOPLE	19
DIRECTIONS TO MY HOME FROM TRAFALGAR SQUARE	22
YOU ARE WHO I LOVE	24
WAYS NOT TO THINK ABOUT IT	27
ONE NIGHT WITHOUT KILLING	35
FOR THE MINIMED 530G INSULIN PUMP	36
4U	38
MEDICAL LEAVE	42
A WASTE	48
THE BOAT CRASHES. DAD TAKES A SHIT	67
NAME STORY	70
IT OCCURRED TO ME	74
COMPOSED WHILE WAITING TO PISS	87
WHY I DON'T CARE ABOUT YOUR RADICAL LIFESTYLE	90
WAKING UP IS TRAUMATIC	92
ACKNOWLEDGEMENTS	95

Erectric Schlock

Aimée Lê

REJECTED BY SUBWAY FRANCHISE EMPLOYEES ON 18TH STREET I WALK HOME WITH NOTHING

I admit
she slid the sandwich
onto the counter so
I could have
grabbed it

But $5.99 is too much for a sandwich

If you think about it
that's a dollar an inch

In theory
you can't trust no one
especially me
having the self respect to walk away
if my coupon is not honoured

Do I have to prove I *have* money

Unlike the 3 guys sitting on
the sidewalk outside the store

But I just don't *want* to *use* my money

I'm not pressing submit
on my time-
sensitive coupon just to prove a point

Žižek said freedom is painful
       —Co-sign—

Do I literally
have to build an organic social media following
in order to get the coupon
for my sandwich respected

At a pay rate of 12 inches
an hour
minus me having to stay alive

The human condition

I put in work for that coupon

I got 3 people to sign up
for the Subway Club ™ but don't worry about it

I should put some of my other problems
      in this poem

A poet recently told me
      everything is political

Don't you think I wish I could be normal too

Walking home with nothing

String of lightbulbs hung up by the lake edge

Sun setting on the contradictions

Just dark enough to see a body lying on the ground

Just light enough to avoid it

I HAVE THE SWAGGER OF A 17-YEAR-OLD

Overheard in the passage to the L train: a man saying "I'm 28 but I have the swagger of a 17-year-old" over and over

Fucking me is no longer illegal. Everyone I've ever known is still alive. I might be wearing a wig. I just jumped a turnstile. I don't have any tattoos. I just made a mix CD with only one song on it. This shirt is ripped on purpose. Everyone is so bogus and I need to inform you of that. I deliberately misspell notes I write to myself. I have a file called "Masturbation document" on my computer and also my e-mail. I made desktop backgrounds in MS Paint of celebrities telling me not to open it and to go back to doing homework. I'm still really sorry about what I did. I'm trying to work on not telling everyone about it constantly. I wish I was joking, a lot. That's why I say "I wish I was joking," a lot. I think everybody interprets this to mean that I am joking, so it's like a wish that works for everyone except me. I've got that driving-on-a-permit swagger. That tinfoil grill swagger. That food-wrapped-in-a-napkin swagger. I'm crying in the hallway. I'm wearing your T-shirt. I think you wanna date me. I only said that because I saw it in a movie. I actually want to stand in a corner and sing the same song loudly into the wall.

HOW IT GOING
after Fiona after Gahl

another occupation
i'm getting fired lol i text josé
who doesn't reply

the workers are walking out
again, the students are walking in,
U-locks on their necks

i'm telling my mom
to wear a diaper to the courthouse – astronauts do it
nathan's case is going to appeal
i still have beautiful young skin

my boss still hates me,
although realistically what that actually means is that I am constantly
compelled to sabotage the work process

getting arrested again
unable to write the novel i want to write
which is just a description of the colour

of trees in summer
in the evening and the million flavours of pavement
as my head gets kicked into the pillow

the 12th floor of the metropolitan correctional centre
escape through flickering lights
i am alive i am in here

not everything is death just most things
my dad actually quit smoking
a vietnamese guy

on the bus told me
whenever i want to smoke
i just drink 3 beers

and boom i pass out

WHY AM I ALWAYS FALLING OFF A CLIFF?

Why did I think if you missed a meal, you might die? I asked, "When you're diabetic and you miss a meal, do you like, die?" Notice I only said that after it was secured in your jaw. I don't like to be a cause of panic. I walk very calmly out the door and then break into a run. I didn't used to run during the day because I was scared that the drivers of cars would see me trying too hard. Why do all these insects, flower petals and ash keep sticking to me? Do they think I am an altar? I dreamt my secret society held an intervention for my behavioural problems. Why can't you all just imagine it's Prince doing it? My name is already an unpronounceable symbol. Why do you always say "We have to talk"? I already know that. I know I have to talk. Otherwise I would just go everywhere bumping theme music off my cell phone. Why do I always float sixty feet in the air? I can only live in fourth-floor apartments. I'm always trying to make love on top of telephone wires and shit. Why do I always spill all this down the front of my white pants? Bleach doesn't even work like that. The pants have to be exactly white to begin with, and most of what we think is white is actually eggshell. Why is that cat staring at me through the window? I thought humans were the only ones who could understand windows. Why is your face so good? I like to set aside time to think about it each night. I wish I was kidding, I do it more regularly than I brush my teeth. Why, the last time I got paid, did I pretend I was a school and give all my friends scholarships? Why did I buy a chain in the shape of a lion's head? Why can't I ever dream in obvious sexual symbols? I only ever dream about bathrooms with hundreds of stalls. I think that might exist somewhere, maybe in China. Why didn't I learn Vietnamese better? My favourite memory of my grandmother is tossing a tiny plush ball back and forth with her wordlessly in front of some plants. Why do I always freak out when someone likes me? Even when they don't even really like me? Go ahead, cars, watch me trying hard. Do you think I am some kind of idiot? I understood everything I was up to the whole time. I did everything on purpose. And that's how I ended up where I am today.

THE NATIONAL QUESTION IN 3 PARTS

1

Now we're the minority in our own city. I'd never seen a foreigner before. When I first saw the Pakistani man who ran the shop in town I asked my mum about it. Now that is alienating. Did you know Muslims put God before their own Mum and Dad? My little girl is thirteen and my son is six and the council makes them live in the same room. They won't get us out of there. About two miles from here. I was born and bred in that town. The council moved a Kosovoan family into a three bedroom house. What about my little girl? The six year-old is hyperactive. You wouldn't neglect your own children and take care of someone else's. Working people pay into it and we're spending billions of pounds on aid for people from the third world. I've paid into that and my father and grandfather have paid into that. The NHS is in crisis. A Scottish girl chucked a bit of bacon into a mosque and went to prison for a year. All right darling, there you are. Fifteen pounds will do. I never used to be into politics. We're not racist. People say we're racist. We just look after our own.

2

Unexploded bombs carried slowly in slings of cloth. Gathering bullets and shell casings from the fields. They turn into stars. We reform them for our side. An airplane rains from the sky. We took it down. Its wings become something to walk over. A man with bare feet balancing a long pole. Songs that grow slowly as a tree, but like the roots proliferate, break concrete. A helicopter painted white. I will come back to you as a pair of crutches. How do we sing,

pulling our artillery through mountain passes. We
recognized that they were Northern girls because of their
shirts made from parachute cloth. Moving the mines without
setting them off. Balance—burial—occasional remainder. In
the tunnels he read until the candle devoured the air, then
composed these songs. The field commander was 9 years
old. His grandchildren were born without eyes. They had
weapons that killed over generations. They had bullets that
traveled through time. We melt them down. We refill the
long cartridges. If you have nowhere else. Which we do not.

3

Someone said, Imagine being descended from peasants for a
thousand years. I don't have to imagine. Jesus also says, You
must hate your mother and father. In many films Jesus might
be the immigrant shopkeeper. In the chicken shop a drunk
man stood in line and tried to reach across the counter at
the staff in their red uniforms. Go back, he snarled. Go back
to Pakistan. Thank you, said the girl to the customer beside
him. Two chicken sandwich with chips. I wanted to fight but
he was big and on my side of the counter. Nate's dad said If
they're bigger than you, find something to hit them with.

MY INTERNATIONALE

Up the slaves in the world

Up to those
               suffering poorly

Warm energy
in the heart filled

        This life is dead

There are no supernatural saviours

Neither God, nor Caesar, nor the troika

Get up!

The damn
of the earth!

Stand up!

Convicts of hunger!

The world will change its base:
We are nothing, be everything!

PECHA KUCHA FOR THE PEOPLE
after Terrance Hayes

[HISTORY]
in the 1980s my white mother clerks for justice archer, a black michigan supreme court justice

when she can, my mom drives his bmw so he will not be pulled over

[HISTORY, AGAIN]
in the 20th century, a vietnamese man is carrying a 6-pack to his car when the actor mark wahlberg jumps him, blinding him with a metal hook

[HEART]
my heart is a boxer but nobody knows how to beat like this nation

[HISTORY, AGAIN]
in the 21st century, a presidential candidate suggests that low-income kids be made to work as janitors in schools / i have already seen this happen / this already happens

[HOPE]
cornel west says the devil is real

[A PERSON I LIVE WITH]
john is paranoid schizophrenic / sandals in winter / his feet are purple and red and green like the flag of some mottled republic

he says he wants to have the dignity of being able to work as doctors pull all the yarn from his head to sell

[A PERSON I LIVE WITH]
graham is autistic, likes dubstep, is more reliable than me and more successful in love

there is no such thing as trash

[HEART]
small tribe / tenement / refugee camp / honeycomb / bully

i just go around everywhere with my heart punching me

[PEOPLE]

chris the master carpenter with the wide mouth, so unaccustomed to asking for help he tries to not to cry. stew, who calls himself a terrorist because if he acted like this and were brown the CIA would already know. nina, my president. nathan, who is learning how to be free.

[FREEDOM]
they have torn the accents off our words so our gods don't know how to find us

freedom is the process of sewing your accent back together, back on

[RALLY]
in the only picture I have of chris, he is throwing a sign aloft the way you hold a child so it can see

the sign says POLICE BRUTALITY: ONLY A BUS RIDE AWAY with a cartoon bus

we decided to have janet draw a bus rather than have me draw police brutality

[GENOCIDE]
there is no day without it, without war, or the quiet war
called breathing

a father has to set his daughter's broken leg at home, in a
splint he wraps himself the way everyone prays: carefully,
over and over, for the same things, for the bone to hush

[TRUTH]
the truth does not want to bleed in public so it crawls back in
your mouth to die

swallowing too much truth is like swallowing rocks

[SAFETY]
i do not believe in safety
there are prisons in its name

i will not be safe, even to myself

i will not speak the way a businessman trots gingerly over a
wet patch of ice

the whole country is that ice
i am putting nails into my shoes

DIRECTIONS TO MY HOME FROM TRAFALGAR SQUARE

I put in headphones and walk into traffic. Imagine the drivers are screaming with desire for me over a horn section. Yeah son, throw that empty water bottle at me. I know what you need. I am dark, infinite, brooding. These guys' pork pie faces are my drum kit. Bash crash bash crash benefits benefits bastard bass. I didn't get smaller. That doesn't happen. I just got outside my body. For once, I'll be the steady one. I put the sound on my back. And if anyone is out there, I'll try again on this channel every Wednesday at noon. Don't let them fool you. It's the same dog as in the advertisement except it's dead and comes in a box. There are infinitely stranger preservatives added to pepperoni than the mind of man can invent. Birth defects aren't funny but they aren't always sad either. If someone had just reminded me that, when measured in potato, fries are the lovemaking and chips are the fucking. But nobody tells you that do they. They just expect you to remember it. Who's that sexless creature who stalks the streets? Only me but I've installed an extra drum behind me for when people ask that exact question. Bon soirée. His fingers have definitely gotten thicker. Not that I'm complaining. Three men sleeping on window ledge of furniture store called Habitat. The store set up to look like a home, lights still on. Many planters of soil. A rustic bench. Art does not require intent or observer. "Lucky to Live Here" cross-stitched on a pillow. Empty. Everyone dead no doubt in a nuclear attack. I lick the dirty sleeping bags, then lick the window. My tongue memorizes the scene. I spit everything out in reverse order. On the train, someone in front of me mentions Rick Ross, then, after a while, adds that a lot of people are probably dying right now. I imagine a centaur composed of Rick Ross's torso and the legs of a thousand corpses. After we disembark, waiting in the road for the crossing gates to lift, a skinny teenager falls in the shadow of his girlfriend and begins to press against her with his hips, as if he is an exclamation point alternating with a question mark. He has been fingering her silently in the seat next to me the entire ride. They are some undulating terror and perhaps we are only allowed that a few times in our lives. It will feel like swinging over a gulch this time, rather than artillery. Please refer to me not by name but only in vignettes. We are almost back now. From where I live, the world is a line of lights strung across a black thicket. That is the airport, and that is London, and that is a rose which in the darkness looks blue, gathering the hedge around it as the heart gathers electricity. To everyone I know, I will be distributing tickets redeemable for one last round of constant apologies while I beg to make out with you. After that it won't happen again. You will be able to remember how it tastes.

YOU ARE WHO I LOVE
after Aracelis Girmay

you, selling trotskyist papers in front of the train station
even tho
it's yr worst day;

you, eating in the meeting

you who keep time; discipline in case

of everyone else drunk at midnight and listening to psy-trance

you to whom the back of the house is a different house

& you still reading Lenin & Hegel where it says spirit is a
bone; in the armchair light darkening forgetting if you ate

& you who can stunt on a security guard like you were
dancing & yell Austerity is a political choice

at the same damn time

you are who i love, filling your syringes on the subway,
making movies with paper maché moons and che and dogs,
skateboarding into a cop,

you wearing 6 layers

& walking out onto the highway like it were a field

& walking out onto the field & asking what is planted there,
is it kale, on the way to the detention centre

& asking what is written on that sign

& writing a flag & holding it out

& making a light

you who stripped naked so they could not touch you

who lay in the rain with me wearing trashbags that night

& who bore me inside your body & walked in the front door, never the back, you are who i love,

you who had to denounce yourself in front of a commission,

who provided a score for your own trial & hung yourself or did not hang yourself in jail,

you executed, toothless, wearing dentures, filing petitions, you are who i love

you at age 92 wheeled to protest for a few minutes, wearing a fleece and a small hat

building a raft, washing the windows & with the same rag carefully cleaned wiping cum off your lover's back,

singing your song, bumping it off your phone,

who handed me an axe & stood by while i took my 20 blows at the same piece

& more i do not know enough to name, more done in darkness & with a rag in the mouth, you i love who couldn't tell anyone it was you, or the children have long since grown up who saw you stood up against a fence with a blindfold on, and only remember every once in a while when wind is trembling in the eaves of their house, you are who i love

who when your voice did not come still mouthed silently that name

WAYS NOT TO THINK ABOUT IT

I
She said he raped her but now seems to not
speak of it or it didn't continue to enter into
shared reality – when a woman says she is
scared of a man, says jacqueline rose, it is not
for no reason – psychology gets you
nowhere, empathy is for the self or figures in
resemblance clustered others ceasing that
are not figures to be here therefore to be
within the enclosure – hosting – jobs benefits
costs – he took over quickly – no recordings
but also, no one to show them to, to share
them with, when someone walks into a
meeting with a tape recorder something has
gone very wrong already – but the already–
wrongness will be used against you, you, in
fact, are culpable, for being here, for seeing
it, for not contributing or – sociopath – he
has nothing but this – she abused him – we
should call their parents and tell them what
they've done – you fucked with the wrong –
you fucked with the WRONG – nobody gon
fuck w my poetry again sd shabine thru
walcott's knife – if you insist on inserting
yourself as a – if you insert yourself – without
asking – or – without asking and without
letting anyone – insert yourself – you're
inside you fucked w you fucked you nathan
should when he spends all day FUCKING
YOU – you should – you should spend your –

you should be more careful who you spend
your – pounds or even people – you should
insist on the impossible which is what – you
shouldn't have done – you are done – come
back – and I hear what other people said and
they don't trust – to x oneself out – to X
oneself to be Xed to be fucked to be really
fucking fucked to be Next (clap – clap –
clap). and the dream of you no as never you
as him he is never you the dream of
someone we all know to whom I refer as in
the centre the web if you know of whom I'm
speaking you're complicit now too. he came
up immediately, I have my journal the first
day. someone called someone a. someone –
a man with a name – called someone – a
woman – a parasite. he is – or – if you are – a
parasite – of the sickness that we are all
feeding from. not to choose, not to limit. and
you are sick too who remove yourselves as
tumours complicit or why didn't you or, you
didn't, go, public, just go, for god's sake
hurry up the idiotic british man yelled behind
me as i glanced back.

II
we should
forgiveness is
we all
we don't want
it's not as if
what does that
for the

at least we can
save something

I pulled the trigger with my foot

In my interior

And I want you to know my interior to know it
like knives if you presume to reach over
which

Bitch I am not the one

Beyond which I cannot save you.

III
I got your back. I got your back which is to
say. I have decided the cost of you is worth
me. But also that the labour you extends me.
But also that. You are not labour you are the
extends. You are not what kills or you are
and I got your back shooting out loud not
the one today is not our day

But I am the extension of what you've done.

IV
When she also spoke it seemed like stopping
I thought she didn't it wasn't it didn't help
first you kill yrself then you move to the
others.

V

There's nothing left to say that isn't sordid –
sort it – sorted. Domestic tragedy at which
we all feel revulsion. Why didn't somebody
do something. Refrain of women thru time.
Do you, actually, give a fuck, about anything.
If so, why. If not, why not. Enough
murderous delusion, now time for the
weather.

My diary from the first day – someone else
behind him, so cheerful.

Sickening to die, end it, don't you, name
inscribed everywhere even where I –

No one. Wants. Anything. To Do. With.

You are lower than the metaphor used to
lower. Far much proto-fascist – if you
disagree, ask yourself, would you be willing
to live there? If you disagree, ask yourself,
would you be willing to live – with him – with
her – with them? If not, why not. If so, draw a
picture and tell us what it's like.

VI

If it isn't true then we've ended up
somewhere worse than expected, a place
where best intentions detonate a pluriversal
anarcho-xenocide. Ask yourself who owns
your fear and why and if he's coming back.

VII
Ask yourself why it only lasted a few days
and went underground the inscription of
names. We found Miguel on a tree.

VIII
Nothing to do with trust or daily life even
motorised and you want us all to sit through
it. And we do. 3 hours on average, is it a job,
were you, burn down, I want you to burn
down.

IX
I dream of killing – not you, him, her – I won't
gratify with the you of the lyric, with the love,
I dream of stabbing him, of bashing her with
a golf club, it doesn't feel good, it's
horrifying to watch something die, but
there's also the alternative, not watching,
not watching as something plural dies.

X
I hate you for what you've done and the
words you've used to do it and to conceal
the crime knitting over like scar tissue, I hate
that I will always be a part of where something
happened and the horror that perpetrators
never see themselves reflected in the shine.
They move on. We burn.

XI

End ownership. End faces. Whatever
happened to B narrativised and imprisoned
in a gallery. Who tells the story owns you. Kill
the story. Death to the story. Who crossed
out my name. He never had to deny it to me
about to beat and drag him until now, funny
the language of threats and the language of
the X'd. It's no good to someone's face. It's
no good to anyone's back. And no one
should know. Fade to blk. Drop.

XII

No use forgetting if that's a labour itself of
crossing out your own name write a hundred
times "I will not remember what somebody
did" and sign practice bubbles n cursing. No
use remembering for whose sake for a
collective formed by the enemy's rhetoric
disassembled years ago the mission
deteriorated self-owned. No use forgetting if
you see their faces and names while you
linger in the half light of the X'd. No use
remembering if you can't sustain the things
you did wrong in the wrong name. No use
forgetting when you might get your chance
on the bus late at night at least to cause
minor damages. No use remembering when
no one remembers you.

XIII

Now is when I'd list your names like some idiot who sends raw emails. But I don't have any. Name names. They say. I know it's a good idea. But that's all they have. Names. And we don't. Or I.

XIV

If I had as many lives as I had hairs. At least one tongue. And it's much easier to kick someone to death when they're already on the ground, that's one problem I foresee. Understanding is a luxury of perps. If even the sun. I could start from any perspective. That's part of the problem. We are in the foothills of a great mountain said someone who didn't understand but was right anyway and dead elephants Hannibal brought. You can't call someone a traitor who was unfaithful to an unarticulated idea, an X'd idea. You can't call someone a traitor if they're just normal. Why do you even exist his gaze suggested. Who the fuck are you then. Would you like something to read. And there may have been no way anyone got to you. Maybe you.

XV

In the un named of all the X'd. In the unseen shadow of the tunnel. In the motorway. In the inexplicit and fucked up in the shadow of risk. In the unlist of the unthere, not the not

there but the made to unbe. There is no
confession. Only the guilty forgot what they
had to confess to. There is just a mark.
Where something was. And then was made
to never have been. There are a million ways
not to think about it. Pick one.

ONE NIGHT WITHOUT KILLING

Dom's dog troubled a man
coming from the east into the park.
*"Boy, let me do you a favor.
I'm a Vietnam vet. If I had my gun,*

I'd've shot him." A tall dark black
man in khakis with no gun facing
a wild-looking white boy with a pit bull.
(Dogs are racist just like people,

die like them too, with teeth
stuck into something.) The two girls
at the bus stop startled. No one
died that night. No sweet young

women like me or pigs shot in a ditch.
No dogs were set on anyone.
The world was twice its previous size,
a mirror had been appended to it to fool us

as in some Chinese restaurants. The man
was terrified. Enough weight of ammunition
having fallen in the war for each individual
to merit a personal bomb. This was not his.

It lay unexploded in a field
somewhere. We walked away,
leash around your wrist.
Your life slipped into you.

FOR THE MINIMED 530G INSULIN PUMP

A flock of pricks

In your stomach

Letters all white
asterisks

You slept on the floor,
an inch above
the ground

While the pump screamed
And punctured you

There are otherwise dead parts
that drink

From the little cure

Here, the ceaseless rhythm,

a tightrope that days walk over
opening
tiny doors as florets of blood,

this miracle

cannibal century you burst into
like a crowded hall in the middle of a lecture

—frail life, flimsy life, thin
as a string of spit

Dispersed and terrified and lit up

Your body

Full of holes
Through which
All this

4U

> *mais le 'i' miniscule avait l'air perdu, comme un erreur, mince, faible…*
> — Quora comment

& wdnt i
take a bullet 4u

magneto
in auschwitz

or miriam in bexhill
(more places
2 belong 2)

morbid also improbable

if the moment comes

we most likely won't b
2gether

as most of the day
we r not

& ppl r seized

& most of the day we r not

& elsewhere
in our heads

literally elsewhere
geist ultimate homelessness

jerry fought off 6 attackers
armed only with an umbrella & his autism
they had guns

fuck enemies
s1 wrote

im honestly not brecht

we r
figuratively

extremely fucked

sth like a pastoral, in stl
a cop-set car fire
within which s1's teeth
will b found

trembling uncontrollably trembling

fugues of popular will

well said

that's perfectly well said

happiness
a vial of oxygenated blood
there is a cost

hard 2 speak & not w/o crying

after all this
will i fail 2 recognise u

though hard 2 avoid admittedly
ur mugshot
adorns my walls

a b-side lenin

all 1 has

i saw
the flag irl
that they made
in 1917

it was literally grey

& still
completely legible

(& wdnt i
also
kill 4u

im not a lib)

2 the body that breathing
must b introduced
2 the body it literally

in december i think
u were on a train 2 ny
i was on the bus
my job as a model
at the cartoon school
the bus drivers radioed each other
that we'd put up
a 2nd tent

this fking world
is ours
if we seize it

MEDICAL LEAVE

1
A Handsome Tombstone with a Yale Degree

You pay to come here
to be happy which means

the name is all over you.
Girls joked "My tits are named

Y and E," from where the T-shirt
blazoned YALE across their breasts.

"The mascot of this college
used to be the slave."

A little brass man spinning
atop a white dome.

On your graduation card, I write,
"Y. N. D."   You're not dead.

Meat turns white when its blood
has gone down the drain with ammonia.

After a week,
you forget the smell.

Joshua is eating out of a bin.
I ask him if he's seen you.

He says no. He sounds pissed.
You stopped giving him cigarettes.

I find you passed out on the floor,
having fallen out of your chair.

You don't like to go to sleep anymore,
you keep insisting in your sleep you are alive.

Two men in a week are trying
to find the Red Cross. I give one

your blanket, the other tries to rob you.
The curb is lower here.

Pollen-bright air near the graves.
The gardeners amble over

the long grass. I smile to hear them,
to think of you going somewhere else.

I see the tablets like bad teeth
standing by the wall.

Yale, the most important fact
between birth and death.

2
Why You Are Called Honeybun

The people who noticed
when you left town
were not your friends
or sexual partners.

Arthur, college groundskeeper,
said, *Oh, you're going on
some medical leave? Getting
all fat and shit?* The guy who

made your sandwiches, wearing
gold chains and a pinky ring,
said *Gonna miss you man.
This was like, your second home.*

Miss Annette, trading flowers for change
in front of the Au Bon Pain
saw you after you quit smoking,
said *You look so healthy.*

You remember what they said
better than I do. You have an ear
for dialogue after walking
in this place you hate for four years

and one unconscious year.
You taught me to throw away a Coke
when I was done instead of stirring it
perpetually and forcing myself

to drink it out of poverty anxiety.
You taught me about privacy, and Stalin,
and you are tender to everyone,
and try to give them what they ask for,

which nearly always injures you.
Spare change or a cigarette
you are trying not to want
seem cheaper in that light.

You avoid your own street
on your nightly pacings.
Julius, the bouncer whom you met
at the gas station,

told you *I don't stare at women.
I just GAZE at them. See?
I'm staring.
Now—I'm gazing.*

He invited you to his club.
You didn't go. There was
nothing to celebrate.
He stood outside

the small Plexiglass window
designed to protect the cashier
after 1 A.M. *I WANT A HONEY BUN,
GIMME A HONEY BUN*, he repeated

until it became your name.

3

Today the Dead Haji Is Not You

> "The detainee could speak English very well and said he had been taking insulin and that he had been captured by the Iraqi forces, held for approximately four to five days, and during that time they had not given him his insulin... I was told twice over the phone, ordered by the captain of the 344th Combat Support Hospital, that I could not transport the detainee, and that he needed to drink water. She also stated that he was 'a haji, and he probably wouldn't die, but it would not matter if he died, anyway.'"
>
> — *Medic Andrew Duffy*

White scuffs on the dashboard. Flowers
in the abandoned lot getting waist-high again
after they mowed it. Delirious tremor of your hands.

Nausea at the bus stop. Ads for online dating.
The fat IV they stuck him with. The width of a pen.
Trauma bore. Clear English. Transparency

in the same vein. Ketones. A punk show:
Spittle/Seizure. Going into his coma, they thought
he was struggling against them. Insubordination crawling up

into his brain. No transfers.
Rattling of ice cubes in a mug.
Ballistics. Bathtubs full of soil. You are both 23.

The medic's head in his arms like a child.
No eye contact. Taken as. Price tagged.
Popped and discarded like a Durex. Pepper-sprayed

and left to die for a movement
he couldn't help. The pock marks
across your stomach, from slender needles. Bee

stings. The involuntary pulse. The nape of your neck
which is always warm. The dusty, sticky mess
of wrappers and Coke cans,

sugar strutting and preening
like weeds by the highway. The
duh duh duh duh   duh duh duh duh   duh duh duh duh   eeep
of your plastic organ. You filling up.

A WASTE

1
We are cycling past
a factory farm & hay
bales, I am pulling
ahead on a corner,
when I realize the
progressive de-skilling
of women is what
makes us act this way.

When you don't
know how to do
anything, when you
are frightened to take
risks, when you think of
yourself as not having
any skills, all you have
is your body, your
appearance, how well
people like you.

You are unable to
extend beyond yourself.
In some cases this is
considered to be a
desirable condition.

2
An injury doesn't
matter or is even
desirable, not an injury,
if it makes you look
better. Replace "injury"
with "incapacity"
and this applies to
nearly every aspect
of life. Appearance as
the dominant axis of
interaction; how you
might appear to others
is what you spend your
time managing. You
don't end up imagining
what you are not doing,
it doesn't occur to you
in those words. But
there are things you are
not doing.

It is impossible to
understand this as an
injury because you are
not entirely well-placed
as a human being. If
you would be able to
understand it as an
injury, you would learn
to stop doing it.

3

It is not a free realm of choice in which some things are leisure. Your 'leisure' is work for another. This inevitably impacts all your relationships. You can't spend 30 minutes putting on your face and 20 minutes taking it off and not feel you have to work harder to keep him. And what is he. Just a signifier that the work is working. An interchangeable validation. Intimacy is secondary. If it were initial you wouldn't injure yourself, after all you'd be a real person.

Your priority is dieting not Hegel. This is a neutral assessment of your time spent. This is why there are fewer books by women in the poetry library. You can't "do both." That's what they want to tell you. Some time on your appearance,

some time reading.
Some time you've
earned money to spend
on harm privately,
some fictitious
priority of yourself as
a subject. "Balance."
Mortification. It's
uninteresting. That's the
sad part.

4

You are not better than
other women. There is
no way to avoid this or
act as if you are saved
from it. A narcissistic
trap that it doesn't
affect you. Those who
say it doesn't affect
them are usually dying
from it. A woman who
has heart problems now
from malnutrition says
it is impossible to live
a normal life because
of all the talking
about dieting and the
advertisements and the
'guilty pleasures'; there
is no such thing as a
normal person.

This is the point: you
can't transcend an
eating disorder. You
can't wear blinders.
You can't ignore the
hollow of armpit in
the tube advertisement
('misogynistic bollocks'
Matt said tearing it
down). You have to
immanently negate it.
The immanent negation
arrives out of the reality
that there are no normal
or healthy people.

They tell you that you
are susceptible for some
reason, that you are sick
and always will be, that
you will never 'recover.'

"It do not matter"

5
I am an extremely angry
person. I didn't realise
that for a long time.

6

There is no one who is
not affected by it. That
is what Hegel meant by
'totality.'

'Good – just one bite'

7

Short story: You died
and we found your
journals from when
we travelled together.
I held them not
wanting to open them
then flipped through
searching for my
name. The light was
deep and golden and I
trembled, feeling a pit
of nausea. I missed you,
I remembered breathing
your hair. I found a
food journal. A page
was devoted to whether
to eat a granola bar. My
heart cracked.

8
No one noticed the
difference which you
spent your time, your
brain, your blood, your
nutrients, your sinew,
your fibre, your heart,
your muscle, your
flesh, your sound, your
electricity to create. It
was an insignificant
difference made
only of you.

9
But behind you in the
mirror was something
else that you didn't see,
dusk falling through
planes of dust between
trees, words to use,
certain smells…

10
A photograph taken
from behind, like
Magritte's self-portrait.
This would be a better
way to understand the
subject.

11

The need to have certain
vulnerabilities which
re-enact a basic struggle
between good and evil.
This way nothing will
ever be too difficult
like having to decide
what else to do. You
can remain confident
that if you'd been given
a chance you would
have done much better.
Someone has a word for
that.

12

The food I eat becomes
thoughts.
I was watching *12 Angry
Men* on the bus TV. It
starts to rain. One of the
most important parts
of the film. It's hot and
starts to rain, because
we are all human, even
when we are asking
for your arguments,
or especially. Sweat
appears on the
foreman's chest beneath
his tie and under his
armpits. To me it is not

a metaphor for social
collapse. It is a way of
touching and living
through the men's
bodies, of putting us in
that room, and when
the bus stopped I was
surprised that it was
cold and a cloudless
sky because I had been
sitting inside an 8-inch
box watching a father
tear a photograph of
his son in half. "Here's
how. Underhand.
Anyone who's ever
used a switchknife
wouldn't hold it any
other way."

13

Kombucha, cabbage
flowers, raspberry
leaves, violets, mint
cuttings, horse shit,
sawdust, bokashi,
biochar buckets,
worm casts, the word
'secateurs,' a mixture
of carbon and nitrogen,
piss, blood, rose,
rue, uterine lining,
hawthorn, bones,
muscle, brain, fat.

14
Small acts that die like
everything is the right
way: 'the end of the
everything' written
meaninglessly across
my two arms in pink
cursive; chive flowers
through translucent rice
paper; this was not for
anyone to have to see,
but someone did see it
and we moved on from
there.

15
"Bees really like it"

16
I don't have to be told
anything. Being told
is nice but being able
to carry a heavy bag is
better.

17
Whisk banh xeo flour,
turmeric, coconut milk
and chopped green
onion into batter.
I like to slice an onion

in long slivers from end
to end. Fry that & any
non-vegan bits in a hot
pan with a bit of oil.

Add the batter to the
pan.

Fry four minutes and
scrape under with a
spatula.

Add bean sprouts. Fold
in half and take out
when crispy.

Plate of herbs, flowers,
nuoc cham, lettuce, beer
in tiny cans, candles.

Your face will taste
good afterward.

18
"If someone went
home and did that
to themselves it'd be
considered self-harm."

I wrote this instead of
doing that, among other
things. It sounds easy.
The cells die off. The

ones it is assumed you
do not want. They do
things like "melt," or
"burn," off something
else, which we presume
is called "you."

"Where do we go when
we die? Heaven, right?"

No. We don't go
anywhere. We just lie
there. "A lot of me is my
body." I have seen dead
bodies and they don't
go anywhere.

19

I will treat you the way
I treat myself. I would
never deprive you. I
promise I will offer you
my lasts. I will see when
it hurts. I won't make it
mean anything.

20

"Hegel's method
is not dialectical.
Reality is dialectical.
Hegel's method is
phenomenological."

I read this instead of
doing that, among other
things.

We were walking
along the rutted track
between barns and
farm-fields and it was
warm still and bright
and you talked about
how you baked for
them and how it was
painful because you
didn't know they were
recovering from –

Painbright to look
away from like the sun
leaving tracks in the
vision.

I wanted to beg you. I
do beg you sometimes
not nearly as often as
I want to. Please can I
have some.

"Men are windows in
the prison cell of being
female. It is impossible
not to need air and a
view."

21

Don't worry. I have
climbed out.

Abstract negation
would envision this
climbing as one
substance or creature
emerging from another,
in much the same way
we suggest our "true
self" obscured by the
numb fleshliness of our
actual presence.

My mouth opened.
Out of it slowly came
the lining of my throat,
punctuated by teeth,
and then layer and
layer of entrails, until
everything inside my
skin had reversed,
like pulling apart a
glove made of hair and
pulsating membrane
and slowly I had
climbed inside-out of
myself until I was the
same as before.

22
I want it, I want some
more.

Impossible to be told
if you eat no one will
want to touch you.
Surely my own life is
the ground for anything
that follows.

He tried to say I don't
remember his words
that if it's impossible
that's a kind of violence
as well expecting
me to do something
impossible but we know
it's violence the trouble
is it feels justified.

Touch is everywhere
– the bee investigating
the chive flower – a
basic principle of
materialism, you know
this, your ass is upon
some possibly carpeted
surface right now. No
one bothers to earn this.

Principle of growing
plants. You don't grow
the plant. The

plant grows. You put conditions in place that assist in this process.

23

A mere person. Struggling along the sidewalk between the height of buildings. To be that. "Death alive in me." To measure all things by yourself. A hand's breadth, a pace. To learn extent, to have an extent, to be extensive in thought and in thought's habitus, the individual in, with, mass.

Line from Bellow about the bus waiting in the scorching parking lot engine "threshing the air."
Metaphors touch, in their own way.

"Whatever goes to the tilth of me it shall be you"

I read that the day
after we raked the soil
into what you told
me it was called. And
covered it with torn
cardboard. Thought has
a reference. We all do.
More than one.

24

A table of contents:
Tell me what to do. You
assume what I want.
You know what it is and
you have it and you are
doing it to me.

The weight of all the
telling. And the way
words and images go
directly into one's head.

Compiled together
we have motives, a
subjectivity – eventually
a life.

Bought and stored or
left out to kill.

25
It is easier to have
someone else's
problems, even easier
to have the general
problem, "everyone
else's problem."

It doesn't fit. I am not –

He said fit was an
appropriate word
because –
Well it made sense at
the time.

She found a circle
of paint laid on the
concrete in a larger
version of Max Ernst's
moon in the moon
over the city which
prefigured Auschwitz.

Shoes go out of style but
people die.

26
You have the task which
is yourself and the
instrument and even
more so when the field
which you are in the

middle of is a crowd.
Thought which is its
own object!

But you have to let it –

Answers have subjects.
Ones we don't want to
be.

27
I ate the sandwich,
it became parts of
my body, it became
thoughts, it became
the sight of your
eyes through mine.
Materialism means
a kiss came from a
sandwich, and I am
that result – of thinking,
turned outward.

THE BOAT CRASHES. DAD TAKES A SHIT

    "I have an idea. You should start with the Malaysian police just beating dad. Just beating him and beating him."
  — mom
    "Or you could talk about all that good stuff in the water."
  — dad

I remember stories
of shitting off the side of the boat
all the fish would swim and   eeeh
I elaborated *and they caught the fish and—*
but who knows what Dad made up
for fun or what I did.
I thought the boat was metal. It was wood.
We don't know who build that.
The boat had a Chinese name no one
remembers. My dad also
had a fake Chinese name no one
remembers. Mom: "All boats
have a name." Dad: *That nothing to do with my story.*

Boat *Not too small like canoe or…*
Reason   when they build the boat
their whole family go.
And 100 people in the family. More
inside. *That consider like*
basement of the boat.

The shoreline is full. They will
be turned away. Sent to the camp.
Police stand like a fence,
with shield and Dad forgets
this word; synonyms: baton,
nightstick, cosh.

The pilot rams the boat in. The waves
marry it to shore.
Let's go. Cannot go
anymore. I carry Nga
I jump down.
Mom: "Was she crying?"
I don't remember.

But Dad remembers the boat
had tipped to the left, so he jumped
over the side where the water
was still chest-high. The police
lay them on the sand
and beat them. *Take about*
a half hour.

Mom: "What did you bring?"
By that time you have nothing.
"What were you wearing?"
COME ON MAN I DON'T
REMEMBER, WHY YOU ASK ME
THOSE QUESTION I DON'T
REMEMBER (Dad stirs his noodles
emphatically and leaves the room.)

some kind
of rice   not enough water

Man get out the international ocean
open champagne

Sit up there
All the wind blow   so good

Because Dad thinks
in location like me, he remembers—
On a hunch, I ask, Why were you on top?

I say I go up there take a shit
I stay up there

I pretend I relative — So many relative of relative

I look up at the moon, Man

Really quiet in those ocean

Taking a shit. Dad's bid for joyride.
Stayed up there
3 days.

NAME STORY

If we are brought into language—
        Language is not ours.
What was your first word?
        Mine was DaDa.

I was Baby.

Does that hurt?
        Yes.

Everything is someone else's, including me.

What do I have in common with him?
We were in the car.
        I don't know what you try to do here.

I told him about Art Spiegelman and he said
Holocaust, that mean the big one.
I don't know what is important about my life.

The heat in the van has not worked in years and the brakes are very bad and he was driving me somewhere and I kept worrying we would skid on the ice.

While I sit on the floor writing it down, Dad starts googling "How to get a good title of your story."

He does not snore as loud as he used to, although sometimes he cries out in his sleep "Fuck you!"

English, the English he thinks in. A language toting its own shame, and pride. Like Oscar Wilde covering his bad teeth.

A single cigarette stuck vertically to the inside of the car door.

He needed help rescuing the turtle.
>   You pick they up.

I grabbed it and threw it in the manmade pond. Alive and slipping into the other side quickly.

St. Maximilian Kolbe is the patron saint of drug addicts. Volunteered to die in Auschwitz in another's place.

Ruth's arm, and the small grey numbers on it.
>   Make them small, she said.
>   I want to cover them with a bracelet when I get out of here.

Kolbe called "Patron Saint of our Difficult Century." He is the only saint with a radio license.

The turtle sleeps with all its limbs withdrawn into its armour.

St. Max raising his arm to take carbolic acid. Patron saint of needle exchanges, of unmentionable bruising, of metal heated slowly over a lick of fire.

The turtle is buried and wakes up alone. There is no species where the parents care for the young.

Neither of our dads had dads. Wars. I don't know if that means anything.

Us. His atonement. That he does not even want to know the name of some days but make sure all the relatives can pronounce.

They did not name me smart, or loud, or even lucky, or brave, the thing everyone tells me I am when I am publicly in pain.

They named me "loved."

It was cold, which in Chicago means you have to dig out your car. Place an ironic lawn chair in the dug-out space.

I do think loving you is like digging a space for you out of the white nothing.
I do think loving you is like watching the empty square form of it holding and dying later.

One night my grandfather fell and broke his jaw coming into the house, drunk.

He was crying, my mom said, and for Grandpa Bill to cry meant it really hurt. But he drove himself to the hospital. (Drunk, my brother says, raising an eyebrow.)

They wired his jaw shut. I could hear him out there crying. Grandma wouldn't let him in the house. She was scared. I don't want to see beer, my mother says. It makes me so sick.

Proverb: The man who does not know how his father died will die the same way.

My grandpa died buttering a slice of toast. Not having seen it, that's how I imagine it.

My parents met in an elevator. Strangers. A friendly question.

When I came to England it was frightening that people didn't talk on elevators. Or that that word wasn't the same. How could I have been born?

Imagine a tiny lantern on pulley strings. Love has a size and shape and depth. To love is like walking into a building and the outside and inside reversing.

Imagine boxes of light. I want to give you a shoebox filled with it. Poke holes in the lid so the light can breathe.

All I could see was a man trying to explain something. A very angry man trying not to hurt us. We were helpless too and me wishing I could make him feel another way, kissing his fitful brain.

When I met you, you were bleeding, having just been struck by a high heel. There was rope dangling from the roof. We set to cutting it down, but you said no, I can't predict what they will do, or want.

Each note itself requires its own name. Asleep, as I was once asleep inside my mother's body while she named me—my dad in a cell—his dad in a grave—my bà ngoai raising children in Livonia not hers until her eighties—my mom sitting in the hospital room last summer for a week without leaving, wiping her lips, touching her feet, patting the coffin as if to comfort it at the funeral, and calling it Ma, which in Vietnamese means mother, ghost, seedling, horse, grave, depending on the tone.

IT OCCURRED TO ME

"Love and Marxism," she requested as for book recommendations which I could not fulfil in the Brooklyn-esque Hampstead shop, lots of upsettingly edifying material for children, toys, I was wearing a pair of someone else's pants which was another reason this wasn't working for me, perhaps it's romantic to argue about whether we should turn Libya into a fuckin' parking lot, for other people, 'intervention' was the trendy academic phrase a few years ago, not the kind we do for alcoholics, some poets are, but you may as well not do it, we were at the ponds which we had to cross through, a half hour of raised white paths along hot rowdy weeds, noisy and hot, sickeningly blank form of 'civilisation'; is it the same in Trinidad, I've only been to two places, on the way back behind a woman with a Nigerian accent: "If my husband hears about this he will divorce me," everyone reproducing sensibly in their mid-thirties and wearing clean maybe overly clean clothes, flowers massive tropical dead in their perfection, bleach, London plane trees designed to not-reproduce, the plot of *Children of Men*, to derive the appearance of life without its inconvenient tendency to struggle across everything, a weed being a flower you don't have to take care of, she was holding the transparent British Library bag, which as I explained was like going through airport security, what had begun as charming was arid and murderous, but in fact was never charming, the sight of the Shard from the hill, I was talking about autobiographical writing and what a dead end it was, I offered bitter and disinterested responses, but I didn't hate pleasure, not the way Miles wanted to with his drawn face and the look of a young German philosopher which was so obscene in analytic England that I could hardly speculate on its conditions, arriving and announcing that the paintings were shit, humiliating us all including the group of Chinese tourists in front of whom I felt implicated in the largesse of colonial pity, we'd come in and fucked still in the pool heat of the room, I an awful swimmer and only wanting to submerge for a brief moment and for the excitement of getting ready, her horrible text message in which it was stated I was "making her the adult" (as for me) his briefs sodden and heavy below the shadow, I couldn't really look at it, I reached down, I felt it was inappropriate, to look directly at… I wanted to do something illegible together in the evening regardless of these betrayals but graduate study is more contemptible than the Shard, a timer shaped like an apple which you set to give yourself breaks, cloth mother, and it was the height of summer but the injunction to enjoy made this impossible, to desire, impossible, she kept talking about love, which was something I wished I'd never heard of, bodies together I was aware of her breasts under the top which was fragrant and synthetic, the water leapt and I hated it, it was uninteresting to me, we had our own lake which had actually not occurred to me, the lifeguard who was equally detailed and jovial watched and gave comments on each of us, delimiting the range beyond which we could not swim, when I next went into the lake the surface was covered in miniscule dead flies, I don't want to turn myself into someone who can be enjoyed, love as the extended form of enforced leisure, I could imagine it well, enjoying not enjoying their own lives, she took a photo in which I knew I looked, her newly slender limbs, vacant, I was nearly ill, ate enough for both of us wanting to be in, damning I'd be of this, but still entirely displaced (I fled) imagining hydrants exploding, power lines falling, to seize the state is to do more, instead of the people falling in the way of the train, an unfortunate inconvenience and one it's difficult to talk about, I was lightheaded and could not tolerate 'love' – enclosure – the enclosure of the pond, the enclosure of sex, for Christ's sake, why be a person?

We ran a workshop where I asked the participants to think
about possible futures and several of them said they liked
the idea of everyone dying, returning the earth to a state
of – after Ali said 'mass extinction' is for poor Black people
– if you think about it, the revolution starts with you – I'd
put poison in water bottles at the bodega with a diabetic
syringe, no one would care, Noah Cohen said in the car,
if I wanted to be an effective terrorist – life hack: if you're
on the can and you run out of toilet paper, kill yourself – I
didn't – sometimes imagining killing yourself is easier than
imagining other things, that is my official stance, it's easy
to imagine what everyone would do without you because
you are in a sense without-you, you are a pressurised unit
that strikes other pressurised units, all of which move where
they're able to, I was reminded
shielding his eyes, staring into them, one of the pupils larger
than the other, the smallness of the pupils gazing into the
light

—the window had blown open and there were water
droplets across the papers he had left on the desk

Sometimes I see and sometimes I am formed into something
by forces beyond my control, and if you are those forces,
how can I
Lying down in front of a very tall building, to make it look
taller
Sometimes
It's not impossible but—
It isn't
What I
But I don't know what I'm saying here, perhaps I should go.

The way we
No
It occurred to me
Maybe we could talk about
I'm open to
Perhaps I
I could
I don't appreciate your speaking in that way in front of me.
It feels as if it's intended to make it difficult to respond.
I am going to set a boundary and withdraw from this
conversation.
The boundary is a white circle drawn across the grass in the
playing field; you said 'level the playing field,' I've eaten
things that have grown in it, three-headed dandelion, I
suppose their genetic faults are mine, waiting in the evening
looking at a candle diminishing, not metaphorical, but
it might as well be, both ends, imagine two people each
holding one end of a rope walking closer to each other until
it hangs on the ground, that is how it feels, or, it is better to,
I, just, hurts
Sometimes sentences break down
The clothesline in the backyard wasn't tight enough and kept
everything flapping back and forth, it looked like a piece of
electrical wiring, hard to make into a knot, things swung
circularly and fell off, pants, a woman and her children had
just been evicted and Matt stepped over their rubbish in the
street, toys, soiled neon leggings, shopping bags, disgusting,
life is absolutely disgusting, our shared life, I asked what
you thought about a suspended sentence, a life sentence, but
I didn't envision us getting older, but it's not good to do that,
it's important to remember you have an age, details about
your life, in case you're questioned or have to tell anyone, I
have a photograph of a photograph of myself as a child, I've
refused to distribute it, I don't want to distribute

everything of myself across everywhere, I don't have enough
self, it wouldn't go anywhere, I'm consoling myself by
remembering you wore my socks when the police patted
you down and because of their thickness thought you were
wearing two pairs, otherwise nothing of me went there, but
perhaps the food, perhaps if I put nutrients into the soil, it
could come up in the form of lettuce or something, at which
point, I could conceal the message inside a sandwich I gave
to you, the message being, I wanted to know, I wanted to be
with, you,
But sometimes people just hurt themselves
David, 21, posted a message in the forum, bolded, responses:
I love you, please keep fighting David, you have a friend,
there are people, they exist somewhere, and someone else
said the best way to kill yourself was to throw a piece of
plugged-in electrical equipment into a pool and jump in
ensuring that the current was high enough.

Later I'd read *David Foster Wallace*, a bildungsroman
about the eponymous David Wallace, a Yale student who
commits spectacular self-harm then throws himself from
the Golden Gate Bridge. The point, as I sat in the seminar,
with a German lecturer who was articulating some fine
points of Heidegger, a student responded that we might
do a Heideggerian reading of Adorno, the cardboard stars
fell from the ceiling of my mind, I crashed to the floor
internally, sweat began to pour from my forehead, the
pointlessness was evident, my speech was being ripped from
my gullet in thin ever-extensive ribbons, I escaped at the
hour, I staggered, began to gasp, there were Powerpoints
of massacred Vietnamese children meant to make a point
about Power, until one of them was smiling, then the horror
was mine, we were holding hands in our hearts and I was
throwing up in the hall trashcan directly next to the white

porcelain drinking fountain with the distinct sense that everyone was looking on although my back was cramping and I was entirely folded in on myself, and when I cleaned myself off and raised up there wasn't anyone, they had all gone out front for a cigarette.

The world yields up much to philosophy, although it is often in the form of appearances of the arbitrary. In evening, then, the houses on Cherokee Street with their slanting roofs and the way they catch the whole pitch of light from shaft to shadow is not nothing to philosophy, nor is the way we move through them, tilting, rotating, like a film camera, as if we are on our way to somewhere else. Now on the other hand if you were to ask me what precisely they yield up to philosophy, I would not say anything. But the fact that this sight itself encapsulates a number of basic problems of perception, of Spirit, of the Ideal, and furthermore, extending towards the social sciences, towards atomic structures, towards biology, and towards simpler questions like why the houses have never looked like that before, why do they only begin to look like that when I am with you for the first time, and although you are off teaching refugees how to speak English, a job which you say you are very bad at, and which I never see you do, but which I imagine you do with aplomb the way you put your beautiful clothes on, the belt with its clear marking of the correct hole (with one on each side for leverage) and the trousers which don't fit and shoes which are a bit nice for the occasion, I walk down the street and suddenly the sunset is suspending some kind of time, suddenly there is a greater amount of space inside me, psychically, which enacts the shadow, which enacts the low-riders & the one empty shop on the corner not quite out of business with a limp flag wavering over the door, and the windows open fully without screens above in what I could imagine as our vacant apartment, but this has become inaccurate, because it isn't, some kids look apprehensively down the street at their own footsteps, one, then two, young men on bicycles with perfectly detailed musculature work their way up the street, pumping at each step, the bike from side to side swaying, and they don't remind me of anything, I see them, I lay a hand on the landscape to my side, it is so clear I can feel it, the most boring branch of philosophy is ethics, you said, but I think it is obviously metaphysics, and to be without any pretence of naming things or that things shine any brighter in the presence of their names, as the young men flee from their names up the street which is the flat purple colour of shadow in the summer but is not itself in shadow. He was like them, a young man fleeing from death. Everything kept moving except for, somewhere, him, he had been chased down. I kept trying to hold my timespan next to his. This wasn't the point, and in a sense, it didn't feel as if he was dead, just on the run somehow, in flight, like the diminishing sight of those two young men on their bikes. The point is, that somehow the earth kept turning past, I didn't heal from anything.

It was raining and awful – raining and awful from inside the workplaces, from inside the flats, and from outside where we were standing under it. I had a sudden thought that it must have been raining everywhere on the earth, everywhere I had once stood, both the narrow path outside the canal where the boat had been anchored, along the glass terraces of the monstrous experimental building across the way, the 'neon entrail' of the post-Olympics construction twisting from below, and rain hammering on the boat's roof, wherever it was anchored, wherever it had been moved to.

The boat had a few difficulties, someone had painted a mural of the sun smiling on the ceiling, it was cartoonish and grotesque, but more than that, a face has to be perceived right-side-up or right-side-down, and it was somewhat disturbing to feel, lying or sitting on the floor, that one was half the time facing the wrong way, the sun was feeling something backwards about one, but also to stare constantly into that crudely painted smile was to pass into the emoji of the real. The windows fogged with damp and the walls were wet and cold to the touch, and the glass of one of the windows was broken. The lock on the door was half-broken, and in order to feel it securely bound one often had to reform the inner tooth of the lock with one's hands. There was also a locked box on the deck with a bit of graffiti on it saying Please don't store food inside, a rat had been depicted on the box saying, "Don't listen to him! We love peanut butter!"; it was disquieting to realize that what one had initially experienced as the voice of an impersonal inner auditor had been heard by the rats as a "him." It opened the possibility that all of the text we read could conceivably take form as someone else's speech, and how horrifying that would probably be.

I had begun to really struggle with art and with words in general. It began by waking up staring at the upside-down face of the sun. But it continued in that it became less and less possible to find surfaces that had not been inscribed.

                                                      I went to take a piss in the woods one day and found the sides of a stand of birch trees had been spray-painted in pink, one letter per tree: F U C K C O P S, and while it was an exciting visual illusion, I'd seen the basic premise used before in a music video, and therefore some art director who read a ton of magazines and went to 'galleries' had found the device, there was no way to escape the derivative presence of culture, this felt even worse than finding bar codes on everything, because someone had voluntarily tried to execute this imagery, someone had subjectively identified with this act, which now tormented me as I knelt beneath the bridge watching my urine darken the pavement. The pavement had probably been inscribed, everything is inscribed, but unlike my fantasies of Heaven as a small child, the fact of having been written on is no entry to a book of life, it doesn't mean it has been taken up into any form of presence.

On the other hand –

When I was sitting with you we were on the bus and the sun was extremely bright and although it was already late and we were both physically fucked and our relationship had been over for a long time, and although later in the evening I would develop a headache, possibly from low blood sugar, which meant I couldn't enjoy anything, for that brief period of time we climbed to the top of a council flat and looked down, not merely for the sake of the gesture, but in an actually submissive realisation of seeing, itself, in other words, the immanence of the things that appeared to us – in this case, some upper middle-class people barbecuing on top of a nearby building, and the fantasy of going over to join, and the fantasy of being a couple, despite what we were actually wearing and who we actually were, sustained a form of flight, rare enough, into things rather than away from them, which meant we stood outside of the building for the next few hours and managed to get through 2 layers of security, although we didn't breach the final door, just hid inside the separate room where they stored their trash, all from Waitrose.

Later we would learn who lived there but for now it was just another building with people wearing pastel clothes they'd probably purchased recently, who probably worked for something.

It's important to remember that this is an illusion.

Autism, bicycles, collective, deviance, environmentalism, feelings (simulated), grievances (nurtured), hygiene, incest, jam-jars, ketamine, libraries, marxism, nature, organising, poverty, queerness, repetition, social work, television, umbrage, vegetarian dinner, wifi, excrement, you.

We were walking alongside the riverbank when I realized the fatal formulation, the form of this relationship is not determined by us, it is determined by the social, relationships are not in our terms, they are a predominant form of expressing the social totality, and strangely, compulsively, at the same time, I love you, we were beside each other, things were passing over us so quickly they seemed like – no – we were passing over things so quickly they seemed arranged in a line by an assiduous set director, an unending procession along the riverbank of alternative styles of clothing and people gazing across at nothing, sitting along the end of concrete, most of them must live, must work, for what, for what.

My next book is on refugees so I must immerse myself in everything to do with refugees. It's non-national-specific – it's allegorical –
There's this documentary – Australian documentary –
How long is it?
I've watched 20 minutes
It's not like five hours or something, because I don't have time

Which part is the material, and who is the thinker? Which piece is an inert moment to be passed over, to demonstrate to another, which piece is to be held in place, which piece is a miniature flag.
Except we saw some flags – some real ones, at the exhibition, made by hand – imagine things like currency and flags being made by hand, they must have been at some point – it was grey. It had been red. On it in the centre were two simple points of insignia, a sickle that looked like a C and a hammer that looked like a T. It was so far from being a logo. The hand of the maker was present. I imagined a room full of schoolchildren drawing the same insignia, all subtly different. A room full of people making the same sound. An auditorium. A city. A continent. A planet.
We have to consider that the sun was used as a sign of the aristocracy, and of natural right. We have to consider that things were perceived, signs were seen, to justify what was done. We are not seers. Or we must not be seers. Or all we

will see is what is. Immanence means, seeing what is there undoes what is there. We have to consider that the planet is a colony now.

When you have spent the day cutting plants and breaking concrete on a building site with a heavy sledge, the few stitches, the insignia, the little black C & T on the flag leaps into eyes denuded of its age, present as an image of what we have done in our days, and what we might be able to use.

COMPOSED WHILE WAITING TO PISS
for Gahl

who can turn anything into an opportunity, through
appreciation, which turns life half-sideways and shakes
it so that – I am trying to refrain from putting any, direct
or indirect, urination metaphors into this writing, mostly
because it's not a difficult moment, I'm not struggling, I'm a
bit cold, when you can pee outside at any time in just about
any place your awareness changes, when you drink endless
cups of tea to keep warm you begin to notice patterns, the
steam of your urine, its odour, the things you take from
your pocket or the ground to wipe off with, the high-rise
condominiums with their slanted and modern appearance
which terrify you and stun your heart, and London is a
hellscape, it's not of this world, the rich belong to a zone
far above yours, a land engineered by AI and floating away
from human forms, radiating red lights and sculpted into
complex polyhedrons, you see them balletically balancing
on one leg to reach the blinds, trying several different ways
to fasten them, because you across the canal, five stories
down, are pissing while staring directly upward at their
faces, their drinks, their lounging, their televisions, their
friends, their clothes, their conversations, their refrigerators,
their invisible toilets, the apartments are entirely glass so
the toilets don't get to have a view, this is something you
never think about until you say it just now. Of all places
to stand or to piss the side of the canals in London is a
terrifying one, one you'll never belong to, because no one
belongs to that maw of inhumanity, the scum floating on the
surface, the bobbling football, the scraped and devastated
flat plane of the dam where all the discards wind their
way to bilge in full anaesthetised light from the reflected
pollution and apartment-dwellers and low-banked clouds.

Somehow it scares me more because I don't see myself in it. While reading Whitman, I reflected that he sounds an awful lot like L Ron Hubbard, thus permanently destroying any appreciation I might have for the bestriding American colossus, chock-full of observations and futurity and punctuation marks and mandatory enthusiasm. Whitman might have been a better drinking companion than I am. I might be a somewhat shrivelled, fearful and critical figure. There are so many things I haven't done. Pissing outside makes this obvious because it requires no talent. Neither does the poetic return to an identifiable refrain that will organise these thoughts, because pissing has been taken up as an arbitrary theme, something I do daily and which has punctuated my deepest loves and despairs, or must have done, even if it lies unremembered in a back closet of the mind, I am suddenly taken back to the rear of some bus, which I rode and pissed in, maybe the coach on the way up from Boston, balanced somewhere far away from the hateful protofascism of my former classmates, who might live and drink in top floor apartments. There are so many things I'm not. To see a line of footprints down the street for example, as it began to somewhere between rain and snow, made me feel I wanted to be that disappearing path to follow, the person having long since gone. Windows over the fence, full of things hung, lights inside, designed just to be big and openable. My home is incurious, the walls of the tent are just plasticine fabric hung over a weightless skeleton, and it shifts as I move or as anything moves it, a dull green colour, on the inside a bit nicer, but nothing to write home about, disappointing and frightening in equal measure, sometimes cosy, there's nothing about piss in this either but I've trained myself to expect a refrain, but there isn't anything to refrain from doing, although I do, frequently, keep myself from becoming another person, out of a sense of decorum, or inability, or simply the scariness of floating off unknown somewhere onto the land I don't know how to walk, the people who live in those apartments balance atop columns of numbers and risk, while I walk along the canal thinking of how awful it would be to fall in, or how to tie a knot, it is to the point where I wonder if our lives are made of the same fabric, the same psychic substrate, although we respirate and digest the same, Žižek and a novelist who wrote a dystopian book whose name I can't recall now both said the same thing about genetically dividing and altering the rich and poor, that the American poor are so fat and ugly and prematurely aged, I am becoming my own species.

WHY I DON'T CARE ABOUT YOUR RADICAL LIFESTYLE

I ate Crunchy Kurls for the first time on Monday. Now I can't stop seeing them. It's like when you have just spent two weeks having sex with a stranger and suddenly every high-schooler with diabetic medical tubing is almost him —headrush, dazzle. People keep doing this thing where they tie grocery bags to fences, and stuff the sidewalk trash inside. They are magnanimous colour, crammed with residue of the day's hands. I am also sceptical of the bags, or their conditions of existence, like, "What, we have shitty public garbage pickup but it's inspiring how people make it work on their own dime? Try throwing raw eggs at the mayor's house. Ya douche" (and then I karate-kick an imaginary adversary, dip-snapping the whole time; the very move which, when performed while riding my bike, caused my foot to lodge between the fork and the front wheel, flipping us both over onto the concrete). Aphorism: the revolutionary wears her helmet and avoids "no-hands, no-feet dancing"; this is bourgeois and for people with insurance. I actually do have insurance; I just don't want to wear it out. I guess that's what I say about my genitals, too. Boom! I've taken to yelling "Boom!" after saying something I find funny, so no one else can. I wish there were a version of medical insurance where neighbourhoods collected litter and old yarn and children's loose teeth and did DIY surgery out of Dave's garage, except, replay what I said earlier. I heard that instead of South Side train service this summer, people were gonna make pedicabs with umbrellas on top that played polyrhythmic Greatest Hits on baby boomboxes except, fuck that too. At one point, when I lived in a tent encampment, I busted my knee on the train tracks. My comrade made a bandage out of paper towels and dental floss. When we returned to camp, an EMT in the emergency tent flushed out my wound, and I, trembling, thought, *This is tight as hell*. We could always have free bagels and 24-hour libraries with that Hannah Arendt good shit, padded vests and group chants. But I went to college. I did have all those things. I didn't sit inside a trashbag for a week in freezing New Hampshire rain to get the life experience of a banana peel. I did it to overthrow capitalism.

WAKING UP IS TRAUMATIC

Says the bodybuilding expert, explaining why
you should eat at least 15% of your daily carbs
at breakfast

It's literally stressful, things are flooding
internally, signals are being sent

We all need help

I wake up to too many text messages

Someone from the union
wrote an article denouncing us

Saying we are too "certain"

Some things are certain in life

I taught a guy at the shelter
to calculate opposite angles
using two chopsticks

It wasn't a proof and I'm not sure
if it mattered to him

But sometimes you need to remember
that truth is physically real

As real as the face of a 40-year-old man
studying for the SAT in a homeless shelter

Sometimes shit just works
even if you can't explain why yet

It is fine to be certain
of that

ACKNOWLEDGEMENTS

Some of these poems have previously appeared in: *Uncommon Core: Contemporary Poems for Living and Learning*, *Litmus*, *Lune: The Journal of Literary Misrule*, *Glass: A Journal of Poetry*, *P-Queue* and *Prolit*. Thanks also to DIY Cultures, the Royal Holloway Poetics Research Centre, the Small Publishers Fair and the 'Fatties: The Politics of Volume' symposium (NICA/ASCA), where 'a waste' appeared and was sold as an independent book.

✦ ✦ ✦

to F who did it with me the first time
& to D with love always
to S who "got" the title & to M who understood "I won't make it mean anything"
to L, "for or against" you as always my love
to M who has been by my side forever, to N who has never let me down — I love you
to the OG Jeff Kass who never stops grinding & everyone from A2 who made me
to G & L, G & all my online homies — if you're reading it, it's for you
to SA & CC & real trotskyist hours
to Sinthome & 76 & especially J my second family
to my actual family living or not specifically the very creative Lê family household & especially S my fellow poet
& to R & R both deceased whose voices I still hear & certain others still alive & maybe others I shouldn't mention or include bc it would be weird & most importantly to anyone who is at this exact moment right now suffering without any consolation — anyone in hell or dying, "sailors in snow"
to R & W & K & RHUL & GH & LDN where a lot of this was written, I hope it doesn't suck
let's do more l'chaim
to everyone who helped
& above all to N — this is 4U

LAY OUT UR UNREST

www.ingramcontent.com/pod-product-compliance
Lightning Source LLC
Chambersburg PA
CBHW051659040426
42446CB00009B/1212